Questions & Answers

BIRDS

Fergus Collins

KINGFISHER

KINGFISHER
Kingfisher Publications Plc
New Penderel House
283-288 High Holborn
London WC1V 7HZ
www.kingfisherpub.com

Produced by Scintilla Editorial Ltd
33 Great Portland Street
London W1W 8QG

First published by Kingfisher Publications Plc in 2001
10 9 8 7 6 5 4 3 2 1

TS/0905/TIMS/UNI(MA)/130MA/F

A CIP catalogue for this book is available from the British Library

ISBN 0 7534 0544 X

Printed in China

Author: Fergus Collins
Art editor: Keith Davis
Designer: Joe Conneally

Illustrations: Dan Cole/Wildlife Art Agency, Terence Lambert
Steve Homes/Tony Kengol, Doreen McGuiness, Martin Knowlden
Stuart Lafford Linden artists, Josephine Martin, Ruth Lindsay
Bernard Long, Brian Mcintyre, Chris Forsey, John Rignall
David Wright, Ian Jackson, Mike Taylor,
Bruce Pearson/Wildlife Art Agency
Oxford Illustrators ltd, Wayne Ford, Chris Shields
Norman Arlott, Bernard Robinson, Graham Allen,
Dan Wright, John Butler, Tudor Art Studios Ltd, Bernard Long, James Field,
Mick Loates, Eric Rosson, Peter Bull, Andrew Beckett, Alan Harris, David Cook

Contents

World of Birds	4
Early Birds	6
Feathers	8
Bills and Beaks	10
Talons and Feet	12
Sight and Sound	14
Food and Feeding	16
Flying	18
Flightless Birds	20
Migration	22
Surviving Extremes	24
Birdsong	26
Displays	28
Nests and Nesting	30
Eggs	32
Chicks and Young	34
Birds and People	36
Threats to Birds	38
Index and Answers	40

World of Birds

Birds are nature's supreme flyers. They are also among the wild animals that we are most likely to notice, allowing us to admire their superb aerial skills. Birds come in a great variety of sizes, from the tiniest hummingbirds weighing no more than a small coin to ostriches taller and heavier than an adult human.

What is the largest bird?

The tallest and heaviest bird alive today is the ostrich. Striding the plains of central and southern Africa, this colossal bird can grow to 2.74m tall and can weigh 160kg. However, it is not the largest bird that has ever lived. *Dromornis stirtoni*, another flightless giant, thrived in Australia about 15 million years ago. It reached 3m in height and weighed up to 500kg.

Ostrich

What is the heaviest flying bird?

Flight becomes virtually impossible for birds weighing over 15kg. The heaviest flyers are the kori bustard (a turkey-like bird from Europe and Asia) and the mute swan (above). These birds average about 12–15kg. A swan is so heavy it needs a running start from the surface of a lake in order to reach a sufficient speed for take-off.

How much does the smallest living bird weigh?

Most experts agree that the bee hummingbird from Cuba is the tiniest bird. It is no more than 5.7cm long and weighs just 1.6g. It would take 100,000 of these birds to equal the weight of an ostrich. The smallest British bird, at 4.5–7g, is the goldcrest.

Bee hummingbird

Why do birds fly?

Flight enables birds to find food that cannot be reached by other animals, while helping them escape from ground-based predators. On the wing, a bird such as the wandering albatross can forage over a huge area, locating the best food in the shortest time. And if the food runs out in one place, the bird flies off to new areas.

Wandering albatross

White-throated robin

What is a passerine?

Of the approximately 9,200 bird species in the world, 5,425 are passerines, known also as songbirds or perching birds. Passerines include most familiar garden birds, such as warblers, finches and tits, and thrushes like the white-throated robin from Asia. Crows are among the largest passerines.

Are birds clever?

Animals with large, complex brains, such as mammals and birds, are able to learn and adapt to new conditions. Animals with simpler, smaller brains, such as fish and reptiles, rely far more heavily on instinct.

Fish

Reptile

Bird

Mammal

Quick-fire Quiz

1. What proportion of bird species are passerines?
a) About a quarter
b) About a third
c) Just over half

2. What is the world's smallest living bird?
a) Bee hummingbird
b) Robin
c) Goldcrest

3. How heavy can an ostrich weigh?
a) 1.6g
b) 1.6kg
c) 160kg

4. How many birds are estimated to live on the planet?
a) About 300 billion
b) About 30 million
c) About 3 million

How many birds are there in the world today?

Bird experts guess that there are 300 billion birds alive in the world today – 50 birds for every person on the planet. They believe that since the first birds appeared on Earth many millions of years ago, as many as 150,000 species have existed. About 8,500–10,000 species survive today.

Early Birds

Birds are such unusual animals that scientists have found it hard to agree on which other creatures they might have evolved from. What we do know is that the first birds appeared during the time when the dinosaurs lived on Earth. Since then, many thousands of different species have evolved.

Archaeopteryx

Which is the oldest known bird?

Fossils have been found in a German quarry of a primitive bird, named *Archaeopteryx*, that lived about 150 million years ago. Although it had feathers and the bones of a bird, it also had reptile-like teeth, a bony tail and claws along its wings. For most people, this is proof that birds evolved from reptiles. *Archaeopteryx* was probably not a strong flier.

Why are feathers similar to scales?

Like the scales found on snakes, lizards, dinosaurs and other reptiles, birds' feathers are made from keratin, which is also the same substance that forms our hair and fingernails. For many fossil experts, this is proof that birds' feathers were once simple reptile scales. They believe that, over time, the scale became more complex, developing the shaft and filaments that make up the modern feather.

Snake

Are birds the last surviving dinosaurs?

Some scientists claim that modern birds are flying dinosaurs. They believe that a few small dinosaurs, such as *Compsognathus*, possessed long feathery scales, which acted like a fur and kept the owner warm. Those with longer feathers and lighter skeletons would have found it easier to leap into the air and up trees to catch food or escape from enemies. Over time, a few dinosaurs developed true feathers and a body structure that enabled them to fly. They had become birds – or flying dinosaurs!

Compsognathus

Quetzalcotlus

What were pterosaurs? Were they types of birds?

Unrelated to birds, pterosaurs were prehistoric flying reptiles that lived at the same time as the dinosaurs. Instead of feathers, they had wings of thin skin stretched out across elongated fingers. Pterosaurs ranged in size from blackbird-sized creatures to monstrous gliders, such as *Quetzalcotlus*, the size of a small aeroplane.

How big could prehistoric birds be?

A few birds reached terrifying proportions in prehistoric times. *Diatrymia* was 2m tall. It had a horse-like skull and an enormous hooked beak for tearing flesh. It could have outrun most other land animals and killed creatures as large as a horse. Fossils from South America, dating from as recently as 2 million years ago, indicate that even larger predatory birds once existed. Called terrorbirds, they reached 3m tall and could have run at 70 km/h.

Hesperornis

Diatrymia

What other early birds have been found?

Chinese fossils from 120 million years ago show a bird-like creature with a beak and fully formed feathers. The animal was named *Confusciusornis*. But the majority of bird fossils are much more recent. These later birds were similar in looks to birds we know today. *Ichthyornis* resembled a seagull, except that it had a beak full of teeth. *Hesperornis*, a 2m-tall flightless seabird, looked like the modern birds we know as divers.

Ichthyornis

Quick-fire Quiz

1. How tall was *Diatrymia*?
a) 1m
b) 2m
c) 3m

2. Which of these is not a bird?
a) *Compsognathus*
b) *Diatrymia*
c) *Ichthyornis*

3. Which of the following are made from keratin?
a) Teeth
b) Feathers
c) Hair

4. Where were the first *Archaeopteryx* fossils found?
a) Britain
b) China
c) Germany

Feathers

Feathers are unique to birds. Lightweight yet strong, their main function is to form wings that enable a bird to fly. Other feathers help the bird steer as it flies or provide a layer of insulation to keep the owner warm.

What are the advantages of feathers?

Feathers are light yet strong. More resistant to damage than bones, they can be easily replaced as they become worn. Flight feathers are long and broad, providing lift as the bird thrusts its wings through the air.

Flight feathers

How can a bird use its feathers to hide?

A woodland bird such as the woodcock (left) may have patterned feathers that break up its outline. This hides it from enemies as it sits in patches of leaves. The female bittern goes further. As she sits on her nest among water plants, she points her bill skywards. Her body position and colouring make her look just like a reed.

How does a bird create its beautiful colours?

A typical bird's feathers are coloured from pigments produced by the bird itself in its skin or produced from something it has eaten. For example, a flamingo takes its pink colour from the tiny creatures that it eats. Peacocks, among others, have feathers with a metallic sheen of ever-changing colours. This is due to the way special feather filaments distort light.

What does a flight feather look like close up?

A flight feather has a stiff shaft with smaller barbs branching off along its length. Barbs are connected to each other by barbules. Each of these has tiny hooks for gripping other barbules. A down feather has hookless barbules and is less rigid.

Barbules

Barb

Shaft

How does a bird keep its feathers clean?

A bird regularly cleans and straightens its feathers with its beak (see page 11). However, this is not always sufficient to keep the feathers in good condition so the bird takes a bath. If it cannot find a puddle in which to ruffle its feathers, the bird uses dust or sand to remove parasites. The jay uses ants as tiny cleaners. As the jay lands on an ants' nest, the ants spray the intruder with acid. The acid cleans the jay's feathers and kills any parasites lurking among them.

Turtle dove dust-bathing

(see page 11)

Which birds have the most and least feathers?

Feathers weigh about two to three times as much as the bird's skeleton and account for five to seven per cent of total bodyweight. Although these proportions remain the same for all birds, smaller birds have fewer feathers than their larger relatives. The tiny ruby-throated hummingbird, for example has just 940 feathers, while the much larger tundra swan has over 25,000.

Various downy feathers

Why is down useful to birds?

Most birds, particularly youngsters (above), also have a layer of soft, fluffy feathers close to their bodies. These act like a fur coat by trapping a layer of air, which helps to insulate the bird's body and keep it warm in cold weather.

9

Bills and Beaks

The word bill means the same as beak. Bills and beaks come in a huge range of shapes and sizes, and are the main implements a bird uses to catch and eat its food. By looking at a bird's bill shape we can guess what the bird eats. A bill is also vital for preening the feathers to keep them in working order. Some birds have specialized bills, which they use as a tool, like a chisel.

What use is a curved bill?

Many wading birds, such as the curlew, have long, curved bills. These are ideal for probing for small creatures in their burrows in soft estuary mud. The tips of the curlew's bill are very sensitive.

Toco toucan

Why do toucans have such big bills?

The toco toucan has a huge bill up to 19cm long, which seems out of proportion for the size of its body. The size and colour of the bill are very important. They act as adverts and tell other toucans that the bill owner is fit and ready to mate. The bill is also a great device for reaching fruit. It is not as heavy as it looks – it is made from a lightweight horn material and reinforced with thin, bony struts.

Why does the flamingo feed upside-down?

The flamingo feeds with its bill constantly underwater. Its tongue pumps water and mud through the comb-like teeth, or lamellae, that run along either side of the bill. The lamellae sift out nourishing shrimps and algae, which the bird then swallows.

Bald eagle

How does an eagle use its beak?

Eagles, hawks and falcons mostly catch prey in their talons (see page 13). The hooked beak is used to pluck birds' feathers or mammals' fur and then tear the flesh into manageable strips. This bald eagle uses its beak to tear up the fish it catches.

Anhinga

Why do pelicans have big pouches on their beaks?

A pelican uses its huge pouch as a fishing net. Flying above or swimming on the ocean surface, the bird spots a shoal of fish and plunges in, opening its beak in the process. The pouch is baggy, and scoops up a huge mouthful of water and fish. The bird then drains the water out. The Australian pelican has the longest beak of any bird — about 50cm in length.

Which bird goes spear-fishing?

The anhinga uses its stiletto-like bill to stab fish. While most birds' feathers are buoyant, the anhinga's absorb water so that the bird sinks. With its snake-like neck poised to strike, the bird stalks fish underwater.

Quick-fire Quiz

1. What material is a toucan's bill made from?
a) Bone
b) A horn-like material
c) Hardened skin

2. How fast does a red-headed woodpecker peck?
a) 21 km/h
b) 32 km/h
c) 43 km/h

3. What do flamingos eat?
a) Fish
b) Algae
c) Shrimps

4. Which bird has the longest beak?
a) Ostrich
b) Curlew
c) Australian pelican

Spring preening?

Cleaning and protecting the feathers — a process known as preening — is vital for all birds. Although feet are often used, the bill is the more versatile tool as it can reach most areas of the body. A bird uses its bill to smooth feathers and to coat them with a layer of water-resistant oil produced by a special gland. The bill is also useful for picking out tiny parasites such as ticks and lice, which drink the bird's blood.

Greater spotted woodpecker

Long tongue

Beetle larvae

How does a woodpecker use its bill?

A greater spotted woodpecker uses it bill to chisel into bark to find grubs. It then scoops them out with its long tongue. It also drills holes in old trees for its nests. When drilling, a woodpecker's head moves very rapidly — up to 21 km/h in the case of red-headed woodpecker.

Talons and Feet

A bird's feet are a set of very useful tools. Some species rely on them so much they prefer to walk or swim rather than fly. Birds of prey have sharp claws on their feet, known as talons, which they use to catch and kill other animals.

What's so strange about an ostrich's foot?

Most birds have four toes. An ostrich has only two – the rear facing and inner toes have disappeared.

Its feet, which are ideal for fast running, more closely resemble those of the grazing antelopes and cattle that share its grassland home.

Ostrich foot   Antelope foot

Which living bird has four feet?

In the forests of Brazil lives one of the world's strangest birds. While most of its cousins have two wings and two legs, a young hoatzin also has claws on its wings. These are especially useful when the chick wants to climb back up a tree after falling out of its nest. The bird usually loses its 'wing claws' before adulthood.

Young hoatzin

How do ducks paddle?

A duck, such as the mallard, has webbing in between each toe so that the foot acts as an efficient paddle. The bird's legs are at the rear of its body to provide the maximum propulsion through the water, in the same way that boats have their propellers at the stern. But while these allow the duck to move smoothly on water, they are not well positioned for movement on land – which is why ducks have an ungainly waddle when out of water. Other birds with webbed feet include seagulls, swans and geese.

Mallard

Why are eagles' talons sharply hooked?

Most hunting birds, such as the golden eagle, catch and kill their prey with hooked claws, called talons. Once grasped by these weapons, the prey animal, such as a rabbit, has no escape. The eagle then stabs the talons deep into the rabbit's body to kill it as quickly as possible. A swift kill prevents the eagle from being injured by the dying animal's struggles.

Talons

Golden eagle

Which bird walks on water?

As it forages for food, the lily trotter seems to run across the surface of its lake home. This is an illusion. The bird is actually running across the floating leaves of aquatic vegetation, such as lily pads. The lily trotter does this without sinking because its thin toes are widely spaced, spreading its weight over a large area.

How do birds grasp?

A bunting, like most birds, has three forward pointing toes and one facing backwards on each foot. This arrangement acts like three fingers and a thumb enabling the bird to grasp tightly onto a branch whenever it decides to perch.

Corn bunting

Greater roadrunner

Typical foot

Is the roadrunner the fastest animal on two legs?

The roadrunner, made famous in numerous cartoons, is a lightning-fast sprinter. Its powerful legs and feet allow it to reach speeds of 34 km/h when chasing lizards and other prey. However, the fastest animal on two legs is the ostrich, which can reach at least 70 km/h in short bursts – enough to outpace most predators, including lions and hyenas.

13

Sight and Sound

Birds need to have excellent vision in order to fly at speed without bumping into things. Most birds also rely on sight to find food – from soaring eagles on the lookout for hares far below to tiny warblers hunting for spiders in a thick hedge. However, birds that hunt at night or live in darkness use sensitive hearing to locate food or find their way.

Right ear

Barn owl

Which bird has the keenest sight?

Birds of prey have the sharpest eyesight of any birds. They need this in order to find prey at great distances. Larger species have eyeballs almost as big as a human's but can see two or three times as well. This is because the centre of a bird of prey's eye has a magnified area. For example, a buzzard can spot a rabbit in the grass 2km away. The peregrine falcon (left) is thought to be able to spot flying birds up to 8km away.

Can a barn owl hear better than a human?

Yes. Its disc-like face collects the faintest soundwaves and deflects them to the ears. The bird's acute hearing then pinpoints exactly where a noise is coming from. This allows the owl to catch a mouse in complete darkness by sound alone.

Do ducks see more of the world than we do?

It has been proved that the mallard (right) can see ultraviolet light and so, it is thought, can most other birds. This means that they can see colours that we cannot. Such vision may help birds identify each other or find the Sun — and therefore their direction — on a gloomy day.

14

Oilbird

Bat

Why is an oilbird similar to a bat?

The oilbird of South America roosts in caves. Light cannot enter the caves so the oilbird cannot use sight to find its way. So, like a bat, it uses sound. First it makes a series of rapid clicks, each of which lasts for about 0.01 second. As the sounds bounce off solid objects, the oilbird is able to build up a picture of its surroundings from the echo. This is called echolocation. However, the oilbird's system is not as effective as that of a bat. It cannot reliably detect objects less than 20cm in diameter.

Do birds have big eyes?

A common starling has enormous eyes in comparison to a human. Its eyes make up 15 per cent of its head's mass, while in humans, eyes account for only 2 per cent. At 5cm in diameter, the ostrich's eyes (right) are the largest of any bird — or of any land animal. However, these are dwarfed by the eyes of the giant squid, which, at up to 50cm in diameter, are the largest eyes of any creature.

What is binocular vision?

Binocular vision is the field of vision directly ahead of you. The better it is, the easier it is to judge the size and distance of objects. An owl's eyes are at the front of its head, and give it superb binocular vision for catching prey. Most birds, like the robin, have eyes on the sides of the head, providing all-round vision for spotting enemies but very poor binocular vision.

Tawny owl

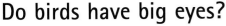

Binocular vision: 60–70°

All-round field of vision: 300° or more

Robin

Binocular vision: 10–30°

Quick-fire Quiz

1. How far can a peregrine see?
a) Up to 1km
b) Up to 5km
c) Up to 8km

2. What size is the smallest object an oilbird can detect using sound?
a) 2mm
b) 6mm
c) 20cm

3. Why is an owl's face disc-shaped?
a) For better hearing
b) For echolocation
c) For better sight

4. Which animal has the largest eyes on Earth?
a) Ostrich
b) Giant squid
c) Blue whale

Food and Feeding

Flying uses a huge amount of energy, so birds spend much of their day searching for food. Most find nutrition in fruit and seeds, which are easily gathered. But some birds hunt insects and animals, which are richer in energy but more difficult to find.

Why are oxpeckers so named?

In Africa, it is common to see oxpeckers clambering over the backs of large mammals, such as buffalo and rhinos (below). The birds are looking for parasites such as ticks and maggots but will happily eat earwax and dead skin. Everyone benefits. The birds get a meal while the mammal is given a spring clean.

Oxpeckers

Can birds use tools to find food?

Several bird species, such as this woodpecker finch, use twigs or cactus needles to probe into insect burrows and drag out the tasty grubs that would otherwise be unreachable. The Egyptian vulture is fond of ostrich eggs. These are too tough to peck open, so the bird throws stones to shatter the shell.

Woodpecker finch

Why do some birds eat stones?

As birds do not have teeth for chewing, their stomachs contain a muscular chamber – the gizzard – which is used for breaking food up. Seedeaters have particularly large gizzards and swallow grit, which they store in the gizzard. As seeds are swallowed, the gizzard's muscular walls and tiny stones act as a mill and crush the tough food into an easily digested pulp.

Which birds act as cleaners?

While eagles actively catch live animals to eat, vultures feed on the dead. To humans this may seem disgusting but vultures perform a useful service, cleaning up corpses that would otherwise rot and spread diseases. The birds soar all day over the plains, scanning the ground for meals. A group of vultures can soon strip a buffalo to bare bones.

Rüppell's griffon vultures

What is the largest animal an eagle can catch and eat?

The largest recorded wild animal killed and carried away by a bird was a red howler monkey weighing 7kg, which was killed by a harpy eagle (left), a native of Central and South American forests. There is a record from Norway from 1932 of a 4-year-old girl being carried by a white-tailed sea eagle. She was rescued alive and well by her parents.

How does a kingfisher catch fish?

1 Like a human angler, the kingfisher must be patient. It sits on a branch above a stream or lake and waits for a small fish to swim into view. Then it attacks.

2 The dive takes the kingfisher completely under the surface. As the bird enters the water, a clear membrane protects its eyes, enabling it to see – and snap up – its target.

3 With the fish held firmly, the kingfisher powers its way out of the water. It takes the fish to a convenient perch and bashes it on the head to kill it before swallowing it.

Which bird uses bait?

Herons, with their stabbing bills and patience, are expert at catching fish. One species has a special technique. The green-backed heron of Japan drops a feather or bits of bread onto the surface of the water. Fish are attracted to the bait. As they rise to taste it, the heron strikes.

How quickly can a bird digest its meal?

Birds live very active lives and their digestive systems are equally frenetic. In studies, a shrike needed just three hours to digest a mouse completely. A bird feeding on blackberries (right), which are mainly water, excretes the seeds less than 15 minutes later.

Flying

Of all birds' skills, the ability to fly is the one we envy most. It enables a bird to cross vast distances, escape sudden dangers and soar effortlessly in search of food. The shape of a bird's wing is an indicator of how the bird flies and provides clues to the type of life it leads.

Canada geese

Which is the fastest flying bird?

The fastest flying bird is the peregrine falcon, which, it has been estimated, reaches speeds of up to 320 km/h as it stoops out of the sky to attack other birds. Just before impact, the speeding falcon brings its talons forward to deliver a powerful glancing blow, which is usually enough to kill the victim outright. In level flight, however, the peregrine may be overtaken by the eider duck, which reaches speeds of over 76km/h.

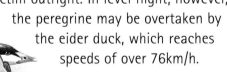

Eider ducks

Peregrine falcon

How does a bird fly?

In flight the Canada goose, like all birds, pulls its wings down with strong chest muscles. This pushes air down and back, thrusting the bird forwards and up. Smaller muscles are needed to pull the wing up again as the bird's wing feathers part to let air through, cutting down on air resistance. The goose uses its tail to help steer while in flight.

What can we tell from the shape of a bird's wings?

The shape of a bird's wings gives us clues to how it flies. There are four basic wing shapes:

Agile: Short and rounded, agile wings are ideal for manoeuvring in restricted spaces, such as deep woodland. Birds with agile wings include perching birds such as finches and thrushes.

High-speed: Short and pointed, high-speed wings are used by the jet fighters of the bird world, such as falcons and ducks.

Gliding wings: Longer than they are broad, these allow birds such as albatrosses and frigate birds to glide effortlessly on the gentlest air currents.

Soaring wings: Long, rectangular shaped and with deep slots between the feathers of the wing tip, soaring wings enable eagles, vultures, storks and pelicans to ride thermals.

How does a bird land?

Landing on a perch is tricky. If the bird lands too quickly, it will topple over, too slowly and it will miss the branch. This dove uses its fanned tail and wingtips as a brake so that its speed is almost zero as it grasps the perch.

Rock dove

Andean condor

Grey heron

Quick-fire Quiz

1. What is an agile wing best used for?
a) Manoeuvring
b) Soaring
c) Gliding

2. Which of these birds flaps its wings the fastest?
a) Condor
b) Hummingbird
c) Heron

3. Which of these birds is the fastest in level flight?
a) Hummingbird
b) Eider duck
c) Swift

4. Which of these birds soars?
a) Finch
b) Rock dove
c) Condor

What are thermals?

As the sun heats the ground, the ground reflects heat into the air layer above it. This warmed air rises producing an updraft, or thermal, that soaring birds, such as the Andean condor, use to gain height and glide effortlessly. Useful updrafts also occur as wind blows against cliff-faces and mountainsides.

Common swift

Do different species beat their wings at different rates?

Herons are among the species with the slowest wing beats. They flap their wings at a lazy two or three times a second. Most birds beat their wings at between three and eight times a second but a hummingbird must reach rates of 78 beats per second in order to hover. At this speed its wings appear as a blur.

Which birds spend most of their time in the air?

A few birds are so at home in the air they only return to land to breed. The common swift is one of the most extreme examples – it feeds, sleeps and even mates on the wing. It spends two years airborne after leaving the nest before it returns to land to nest for the first time.

19

Flightless Birds

Although flying offers great advantages, it uses a vast amount of energy and food. Many birds have given up flying to save this energy. But being flightless is risky as it is harder to escape from predators. A few flightless birds have evolved to be very large in order to survive.

How does an emu escape its enemies?

The emu, like most flightless birds that live solely on land, is an exceptional runner. With its relatives, the ostrich, rhea and cassowary, it can out-pace the fastest hunters. And all these birds can deliver a vicious kick if an enemy gets too close. In Australia there may be over one million emus in the wild.

Emu

What do flightless birds use their wings for?

Even though they do not fly, flightless birds still have wings. The large, fast running birds, such as ostriches, use their wings to aid their balance as they sprint at high speeds. They also flap their wings up and down to fan themselves in order to cool down. The kiwi makes less use of its wings. Just 4–5cm long, the wings are held tightly against the bird's body and are difficult to see. The kiwi's feathers are unlike those of other birds and seem much more like a mammal's fur.

What does a kiwi eat?

A native of New Zealand, the kiwi (above) eats soil-dwelling creatures, such as spiders and beetles. It hunts at night and has poor sight so finds food using smell and by probing with its sensitive bill. The bird can also hear animals moving in the soil. The kiwi's diet and behaviour are similar to those of the badger, a common mammal in many parts of the world. The badger does not occur in New Zealand so the kiwi has little competition for its food.

Why has the cassowary got a bad reputation?

If cornered, this 1.7m tall bird jumps up and strikes out with its huge, blade-like claws. There are several records of people in New Guinea and Australia dying from injuries caused by these powerful birds. Other birds known to have killed people include ostriches and even mute swans.

Where does the rhea live?

Reaching 1.3m tall, the rhea (right) is the largest bird found in either North or South America. It lives mainly on the pampas grasslands of Argentina where, in winter, it gathers in impressive flocks of over 100 birds. The rhea mainly eats roots, fruits and leaves but will also snatch up small creatures, such as lizards.

What is a kakapo?

The kakapo is the world's only flightless parrot. It is also the heaviest. Like the kiwi, it is a native of New Zealand. It used to be found all over the country but in modern times has been driven out of all but the remotest islands by rats and cats. The kakapo is now one of the world's rarest birds with fewer than 100 individuals left in the wild.

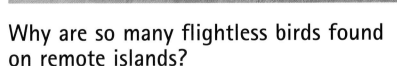

Dodo

Why are so many flightless birds found on remote islands?

Although a few are found on the mainland and most of these are very large, the majority of the world's flightless birds are found on remote islands. These birds originally flew to the islands, found there were no predators and evolved to become flightless because there was no need to fly to escape danger. But once humans discovered the islands, birds such as the dodo were at the mercy of hungry sailors.

Quick-fire Quiz

1. Which mammal does the kiwi behave like?
a) Cat
b) Badger
c) Rat

2. What does a rhea eat?
a) Fish
b) Roots
c) Other birds

3. What is the cassowary's most savage weapon?
a) Its feet
b) Its beak
c) Its wings

4. How many emus are thought to live in Australia?
a) About 1,000
b) About 100,000
c) Over one million

Migration

Humans have long been fascinated by the way certain birds appear just for summer – or winter – then disappear only to return a year later. This movement is known as migration. Typically, a migrating bird travels between one region that offers winter feeding, and another that provides the ideal conditions for summer breeding.

Why do some birds fly in V-formations?

Birds such as geese migrate in V-formations (below). This saves energy for the whole flock. The leading bird cuts through the air creating a slipstream – this exerts a pulling force on the bird behind it. This slipstream carries right to the tail of the formation so that each bird, except the leader, gets help from the bird in front of it. Every bird takes its turn leading so that no bird becomes exhausted.

Humpback whale

How do birds survive long migrations?

Before migrating, birds feed heavily to build up layers of fat in their bodies, which provide fuel for a long journeys. This increases the bird's total bodyweight by 30–45 per cent. The dunlin, a tiny wader, increases its weight from 50g to 110g. It can fly 4,000km non-stop. Long flights enable tiny birds to cross barriers such as the Sahara Desert and Mediterranean Sea.

Dunlin

Why join a flock?

Birds join flocks for their own safety. In Europe, for example, tits of various species feed together. As the flock flits from tree to hedgerow, an attacking sparrowhawk finds it difficult to select a single victim. And because the flock has so many pairs of watchful eyes, the hawk is less likely to be able to surprise the tits. The extra pairs of eyes also help the birds find more food.

What other animals migrate?

Many animals migrate and they do so for the same reasons as birds. The monarch butterfly flies over 3,000km from Canada to Mexico each year. Humpback whales make annual trips between summer breeding grounds in warm seas and winter feeding grounds in the Arctic or Antarctic.

Where do swallows and swifts go?

Swifts and swallows spend most of the year feeding on the plentiful insects of central and southern Africa. However, in the dry season there is less food so the birds fly to Europe. They time this to coincide with the European summer when insects are abundant. The birds spend three months raising young before returning to Africa.

Swift

Quick-fire Quiz

1. How are fat deposits used during migration?
a) For fuel
b) For warmth
c) For speed

2. Why do birds use V-formations?
a) To hunt birds
b) To make patterns
c) To save energy

3. Why do birds watch the stars?
a) To know their horoscope
b) To find their way
c) To find partners

4. How far does an Arctic tern fly each year?
a) Up to 5,000km
b) Up to 50,000km
c) Up to 500,000km

How do birds find their way?

Small birds fly at night to keep cool – they use the position of the stars to find their way. Larger birds, such as birds of prey, fly on hot air currents provided by the Sun's heat. They fly by day using the Sun and landmarks as guides. Birds such as homing pigeons find their way using an in-built compass in their brains that aligns with the Earth's magnetic field.

Arctic tern

Which bird flies furthest?

The Arctic tern is a champion traveller. It breeds around the Arctic Ocean before flying to Antarctica – 16,000km away. With foraging trips included, the tern travels up to 50,000km a year. In its 25-year lifespan, the bird will have flown the equivalent of travelling to the Moon and back!

Stars

Sun

Earth's magnetic field

Landmarks

Homing pigeon

Surviving Extremes

Birds are extremely versatile and have exploited almost every habitat on Earth. This includes many areas inhospitable to humans, such as frozen Antarctica or the fiercely hot Sahara Desert. But each species must have special abilities in order to survive.

What do ocean-going birds drink?

Salt water is undrinkable, so birds that live at sea, such as albatrosses, puffins, gulls and petrels, get all of their fresh water from the animals – usually fish or squid – that they eat. However, the birds still absorb a great deal of salt. To get rid of this, the birds have a special gland at the base of their beak that gets rid of the excess. The birds often 'sneeze' to expel the salt.

How does the sandgrouse prevent its chicks from dying of thirst?

The sandgrouse, which lives in the dry parts of Africa and Asia, nests in remote areas to avoid predators. This means it is far away from water. For an adult this is no problem as it can fly great distances. However, to provide water for newly born chicks, the male soaks his breast and belly feathers until they are saturated. He then flies back to the nest and allows the chicks to suckle moisture from his feathers.

Pallas' sandgrouse

Atlantic puffin

How do birds survive hot and cold?

In hot weather, a bird flattens its feathers so that heat is conducted away from its body. The bird also pants to let moisture evaporate from its mouth. In winter, a bird keeps warm by ruffling up its feathers to enlarge the layer of insulation around its body. Shivering also helps by increasing oxygen consumption. This burns up fat reserves and creates heat. On a severe winter's night, a small bird, such as a wren, loses up to half its bodyweight in this way.

Common wren

Emperor penguins

Which birds are at home underwater?

Of all birds, penguins are the best adapted to swim
at high speeds underwater. Powered by their wings, which act
as broad flippers, these streamlined birds reach
speeds of up to 25 km/h as they chase fish. In the
northern hemisphere, penguin-like
birds called auks, such as puffins and guillemots, also use their
wings to swim underwater. Unlike penguins these birds can also fly.

How does a white outfit help?

Many birds and animals live in areas where snow
covers the ground in winter. For hunters and
hunted alike, being able to blend into the snow
can be a life-saver. The ptarmigan, a type of grouse,
is brown in summer but turns white as the winter
snow falls enabling it to hide from its enemy, the
Arctic fox. The snowy owl is white all-year round.
As it attacks from the air, it blends into the pale
sky of its Arctic home whatever the time of year.

Arctic fox   Ptarmigan

Snowy owl

Which birds live mostly on the open ocean?

Humans can only explore the open ocean in a sturdy boat loaded with
plenty of food and water. Birds such as petrels and albatrosses,
however, find all they need on the high seas and rarely
come ashore. They feed on live fish and any dead animals
that float to the surface. Their superb sense of
smell means they can detect rotting
whale carcasses up to
30km away.

Storm petrels

Quick-fire Quiz

1. Which northern
hemisphere birds
resemble penguins?
a) Hawks
b) Auks
c) Petrels

2. Over what range
can an albatross
smell food?
a) 10km
b) 20km
c) 30km

4. How does a
male sandgrouse
carry water?
a) In his beak
b) In his belly
c) In his feathers

4. How fast can a
penguin swim?
a) 25 km/h
b) 30 km/h
c) 40 km/h

Birdsong

Although birds are sometimes hard to spot, their songs are all around us. Some birds have simple one-note calls or harsh screams, others have long, melodious trills, warbles or whistles. Birds use their calls to attract a mate, keep in contact with each other and to warn other birds of danger.

What is an alarm call?

If a small bird spots an attacking hawk, it emits a high-pitched call and then heads for cover. The call is difficult for the hawk to trace but all other birds nearby, whatever species, understand its meaning and they emit similar calls before falling quiet and hiding. The stonechat, like most birds, greets ground-based enemies, such as a cat, with a raucous clamour, telling the attacker that it has been spotted.

Stonechat

When do birds sing?

Birds are most vocal at the start of the breeding season. A male, such as this bluethroat, establishes a territory by finding a vantage point from which to show off and sing. His song has two messages. To rival males he announces 'go away, this place is mine', while to females he says 'be my mate'. Females choose males with the strongest songs or the greatest variety of melodies.

Bluethroat

Which birds can copy the human voice?

Several species of birds have such well-developed vocal apparatus that they can reproduce the human voice. The African grey parrot and the Indian hill mynah are both experts. However, the record-holder is the budgerigar. One bird is in the records books with a vocabulary of over 1,700 words.

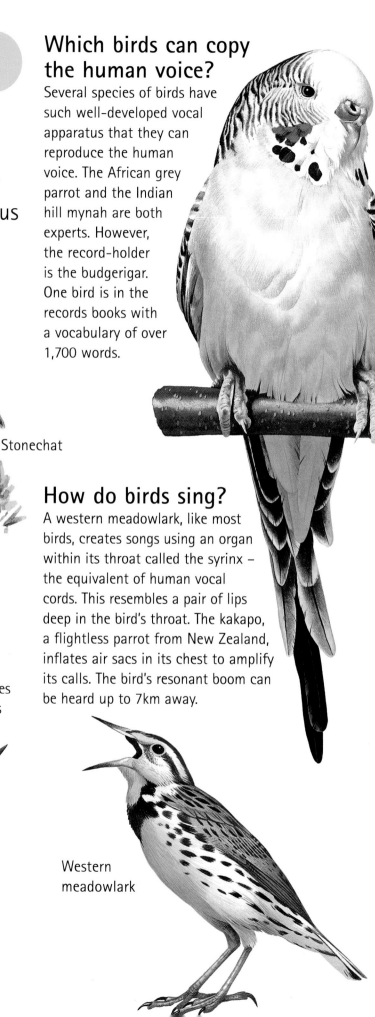

How do birds sing?

A western meadowlark, like most birds, creates songs using an organ within its throat called the syrinx – the equivalent of human vocal cords. This resembles a pair of lips deep in the bird's throat. The kakapo, a flightless parrot from New Zealand, inflates air sacs in its chest to amplify its calls. The bird's resonant boom can be heard up to 7km away.

Western meadowlark

Budgerigar

Nightingale

Why are woodland birds' songs so complex?

Birds that live in dense woodland, such as wrens and nightingales, have few vantage points from which to show off. They can also be ambushed easily if they do show themselves. Therefore, they hide in deep cover and rely on richer, more melodious songs to tell other birds who they are. The complex song conveys an enormous amount of information about the singer's health and readiness to breed.

What is the marsh warbler famous for?

Marsh warbler

The marsh warbler, a rather small, rare, secretive bird, is a remarkable mimic of other birds. A male can imitate up to 100 different species with about half from its European breeding range and the other half from its African winter home. The warbler spends so much time singing other birds' songs that its own song is hard to distinguish. Australia's lyrebird, another great mimic, can imitate a burglar alarm, chainsaw and many other mechanical devices.

What is the dawn chorus?

In many parts of the world, birds, including cockerels, greet the coming dawn with a cacophony of sound. The reasons for this outburst are not fully understood. Some experts claim that birds sing to warm up for the coming day's activity, and that the song re-establishes territories and bonds between males and females after the night's rest. Others believe that the chorus is something birds do to kill time until the sun rises and it becomes warm enough for insects and other creatures that birds eat to venture out. Perhaps birds sing for joy. No one knows for certain.

Quick-fire Quiz

1. How far can a kakapo's call carry?
a) 1km
b) 7km
c) 100km

2. Which of these is the greatest bird imitator?
a) Cockerel
b) African grey parrot
c) Marsh warbler

3. Which body part do birds use to make their songs?
a) Beak
b) Foot
c) Throat

4. Why do male birds sing?
a) To attract females
b) To distract enemies
c) To beg for food

Displays

At the start of the breeding season, birds begin a frenzied search for mates and nest sites. Males, in particular, flaunt their plumage to attract females while making aggressive displays to drive off rivals.

Blue bird of paradise

White egrets

Satin bowerbirds

What is a bird of paradise?

Found mostly in Papua New Guinea, birds of paradise have some of the most glorious feathers of all. The males show these off by either dancing on a communal stage – a special branch or patch of ground – or by contorting their bodies. The blue bird of paradise flaunts his extravagant feathers by hanging upside down.

Do birds give presents?

Many male birds give females presents of food. This impresses the female, showing her that the male will be able to supply enough food for her chicks during the breeding season. It also strengthens the bond between the birds and provides the female with the energy needed for producing eggs. A male may also offer pieces of nesting material as is the case with these egrets.

Which bird is a decorator?

The male bowerbird does not make displays with his feathers. Instead, in order to attract a mate, he arranges bright objects, such as berries and petals, in a twig tent. This construction is known as a bower.

Why are female birds often duller than males?

Males, like this golden oriole (right) need bright, noticeable plumage in order to impress mates and discourage rivals.
But such bright colours also attract predators. The female, sitting on a clutch of eggs, is very vulnerable. Unlike the male, she cannot necessarily fly away. So duller colours help camouflage her against the nest and surrounding vegetation.

Male

Female

Why does the great crested grebe dance with its mate?

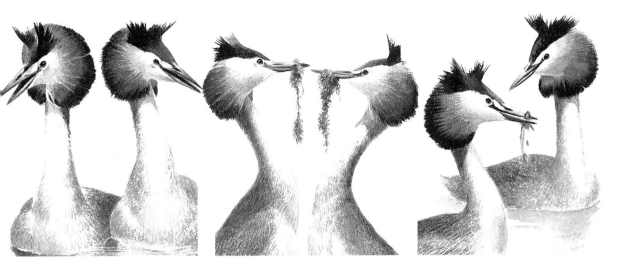

1 In some species, females select their male partners by how well they dance. Great crested grebes swim up to one another and twist their heads from side-to-side in unison.

2 If the female accepts the male's dancing technique, the two birds perform a weed dance. This involves both birds undertaking an elegant dance while carrying water weed.

3 With the bond between the two grebes firmly established, they mate. The male then delicately offers the female gifts of food to give her energy for laying eggs.

What is the frigate bird's pouch used for?

In the breeding season, which is the only time this ocean wanderer comes ashore, the male frigate bird develops an inflatable, red pouch. Once he has found a nest-site he inflates his pouch with air to bursting point and flaunts it at passing females, hoping to attract one of them. However, he may be attacked by a rival male hoping to burst the pouch and steal his nest-site.

Which bird has the most impressive outfit?

Well-known in zoos and parks across the world, the male peafowl, or peacock (right), possesses a great train of feathers that he erects into a dramatic fan of metallic 'eyes'. He then rustles this display to attract the attention of the duller female. Peafowl come from India, Sri Lanka and Pakistan.

Quick-fire Quiz

1. Which material do great crested grebes dance with?
a) Water weed
b) Petals
c) Berries

2. Where does the peacock come from?
a) India
b) Papua New Guinea
c) England

3. What does a frigate bird use to attract a mate?
a) A fish
b) An inflatable pouch
c) A red balloon

4. Which bird dances on a stage?
a) Bird of paradise
b) Peacock
c) Golden oriole

Nests and Nesting

A major way that birds differ from other animals – with the exception of mammals – is the care they take over rearing young. Nesting is the most obvious example of this – the building of a secure home in which to brood eggs and raise chicks. These 'homes' range from simple scrapes in the ground to intricate pouches woven from spiders' webs.

Which birds build the largest and smallest nests?

Built from twigs, bald eagle nests weigh up to three tonnes. However, the malleefowl's incubation mounds (left) can contain over 50 tonnes of earth – the largest nests of all birds. In contrast, the vervain hummingbird's nest is no larger than a halved table tennis ball.

What are nests made from?

A basic nest consists of large twigs to makes the frame with smaller twigs in between to bind it all together. The inner bowl of a nest, such as that of the snow finch, is lined with soft feathers. Birds are resourceful and use all kinds of material in their nests, including string, plastic, old stockings and wire.

Snow finch

Which bird stitches its nest together?

The tailorbird is one of the most skilled nest builders in the world. Its beak is long and thin like a needle, and the bird uses this tool to stitch two leaves together in order to create a pouch for its eggs. The tailorbird uses spiders' silk as thread, which for its size is one of the strongest materials in the world.

Which birds don't bother with nests?

Not all birds build elaborate nests. The fairy tern simply lays its egg on the branch of a tree, while the Arctic tern (left) scrapes a hollow out of pebbles. Cuckoos and a few species of duck lay eggs in the nests of other birds and let these foster-parents do the work of rearing the young. Falcons, among others, may use the abandoned nests of pigeons or crows for their own use. The dikkop, from Africa, nests on the sun-dried droppings of hippos.

Quick-fire Quiz

1. What are nests for?
a) To protect eggs
b) To cool eggs
c) To store food

2. Which bird uses its bill as a needle?
a) Ovenbird
b) Bald eagle
c) Tailorbird

3. Which bird constructs the largest nest?
a) Dikkop
b) Malleefowl
c) Bald Eagle

4. Which bird has the most valuable nests?
a) Cave swiftlet
b) Gannet
b) Fairy tern

Does the ovenbird cook its eggs?

No. The rufus ovenbird, a native of South America, is named after the shape of its nests, which resemble the traditional ovens of Paraguay and Argentina. The bird creates these out of a mixture of straw, mud and cow dung. The sun dries the 'oven' until it is so hard that no predator can break it open. Other birds that build nests out of mud include rock fowl, swallows and martins.

Which bird builds its nest out of spit?

Swifts and swiftlets have large saliva glands. These produce glue that holds nest material – mud and straw – together. Cave swiftlets, from southeastern Asia make their entire nest from saliva. Local people collect and sell the nests to restaurants where they are served up as 'birds' nest soup'. The high prices paid make them the world's most valuable nests.

Why do some birds nest close together in colonies?

About 13 per cent of all birds breed in colonies but this includes 93 per cent of seabirds, such as these gannets (right). The main advantage of a colony is that it acts as a centre of information where individuals can find out from others where are the best feeding areas. The greater numbers also mean that there are more sets of eyes on the look-out for predators. If the colony is attacked, the birds can work together to repel intruders.

Eggs

A bird's egg is one of nature's greatest wonders. Delicate, smooth and often beautifully patterned, it seems too fragile for the job it does. But, tended by the parents, the egg provides all the security and food the baby bird needs until it is big enough to hatch out and face the world.

What are the yolk and the white for?

The yolk provides food for the growing embryonic chick. The white contains the chick's precious water supply as well as extra protein. The eggs of some birds, such as chickens and quail, contain a large amount of yolk. This enables the chick to develop very fully while still inside the shell. When it finally emerges, the chick is well developed and more independent than the helpless young of most birds.

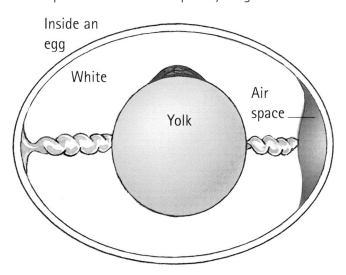

Inside an egg

White

Yolk

Air space

Why don't birds give birth to live babies – just like humans do?

If birds carried their young inside their bodies before giving birth – just as humans do – they would be too heavy to fly. Instead, a female produces an egg inside her body and lays it the moment it is produced. The young bird then begins its development inside the egg, while the mother is free to fly and find food.

How are eggs produced?

Male and female birds mate, fertilizing cells inside the female's body. These cells will develop into the chick. The female then produces yolk and white to nourish the chick, and surrounds them all with a shell formed from crystal-like secretions from her womb. The womb walls may also secrete pigments that pattern the egg and help camouflage it. Some birds, such as penguins, lay just a single egg per breeding attempt. Others, such as the grey partridge, lay clutches of up to 20 eggs or more.

Golden eagle   Chaffinch   Hoopoe

What is incubation?

This is the process whereby the parent birds keep their eggs at just the right temperature for the young bird to develop inside. Most birds, such as the guillemot (right) sit on their eggs to keep them warm. The malleefowl, however, covers its eggs with vegetation and then a large mound of sandy soil. As the vegetation rots, it produces heat, which incubates the eggs.

Is it easy for a chick to escape its egg?

Eggshell is a tough obstacle for a baby bird to break through as it hatches. While in the egg, the chick grows a tooth on the top of its bill, which it uses to punch a hole in the shell. But it is a slow process and it may be a whole day before the chick emerges. Ostrich chicks face the hardest task as they have to break out of the largest, toughest eggs of all birds.

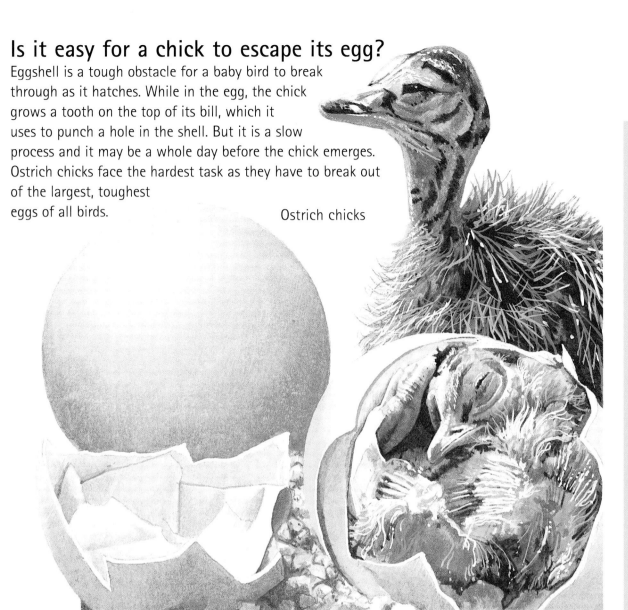

Ostrich chicks

How quickly do chicks develop inside eggs?

The chicks of some small birds, such as the hawfinch, hatch out in as little as 10 days. However, the flightless kiwi of New Zealand has an incubation period of over 80 days. The chicken takes about 21 days before it is ready to hatch.

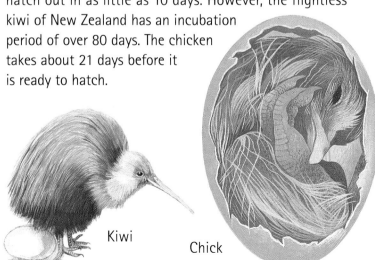

Kiwi

Chick

What other animals lay eggs?

Most animals lay eggs, including insects, spiders and other invertebrates. Fish, amphibians and reptiles also lay eggs, although many species of each give birth to live young. Mammals are the only animals that do not lay eggs – with two notable exceptions – platypuses (below) and echidnas of Papua New Guinea and Australia.

Chicks and Young

Most chicks are helpless, and need constant care and attention from their parents if they are to avoid being eaten by predators. Birds use different methods to ensure their young survive. One of the most popular is to rear young in inaccessible nests until the chicks grow feathers and learn to fly. The swallow (above left) employs this technique.

Can baby birds fly?
Most baby birds need to grow further after hatching before they develop the feathers and the strength to fly. While this takes a few weeks for most birds, such as the eclectus parrot (above), the wandering albatross chick takes 40 weeks to grow sufficiently.

How do cuckoos use foster parents?

1 The female cuckoo lays an egg in the nest of another species in the hope that the nest owners will raise the cuckoo chick as their own. Before laying, she removes one of the original eggs to hide her deception. She then finds other nests to lay eggs in.

2 The nest owners, in this case a pair of reed warblers, are easily fooled, and incubate all the eggs. The cuckoo chick hatches first. As soon as the parents leave the nest, it pushes all of the other warbler eggs out of the nest so that only it remains.

3 The warblers feed the chick as if it were their own. As it now has no competition for food, the ever-hungry chick grows quickly, soon dwarfing its tiny foster parents. They may even have to jump on to the chick's back in order to reach its gaping mouth.

Quick-fire Quiz

1. Which bird carries its young on its feet?
a) Emperor penguin
b) Pelican
c) Swallow

2. How many times a day does a great tit hunt for food?
a) 100
b) 500
c) 900

3. What do pelicans feed their young?
a) Worms
b) Fish
c) Seeds

4. Which bird uses foster parents?
a) House crow
b) Cuckoo
c) Parrot

Are some birds more protective of their young than others?

Most baby birds are born helpless and need to be fed, protected and kept warm by their parents. The great crested grebe (above) ferries its young on its back until they are strong enough to paddle on their own. The great tit may make 900 feeding trips a day in order to rear its young. However, the malleefowl plays no part in raising its chicks. Its young are well-developed and can find food and fly within 24 hours of hatching.

How does a young pelican grab a meal?

As soon as the parent bird returns from a fishing trip, the greedy chick pesters it for food. The moment the adult opens its beak, the young pelican reaches deep into the massive pouch to feast on a meal of fish, which the adult has already partially digested.

How do penguin chicks survive the cold?

In the Antarctic, pairs of emperor penguin parents (right) brood their single chick on their feet for 45–50 days so that it does not touch the ice and instantly freeze to death.

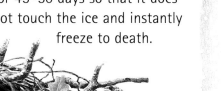

What do baby birds eat?

Some chicks, like these house crow nestlings (above), readily eat the same undigested food as their parents, such as a juicy worm. Others can take food only after the parents have partially digested it. As they grow, they progess onto more solid food, just like humans.

Birds and People

Birds, like many animals, have often been exploited for our own pleasure and profit. Some we keep as pets, others, such as carrier pigeons, perform jobs for us. A few species provide us with food. But we do not have it all our own way. Some birds have adapted to take advantage of human activities – and not always to our benefit.

Which birds are successful at exploiting humans?

House sparrow

While many birds are threatened by human activities, the house sparrow and, most commonly, the feral pigeon seem to thrive on human contact. They both find plenty of food and nesting sites in cities. The feral pigeon is descended from the coast-dwelling rock dove but has substituted urban buildings for its usual cliff-top nest sites.

Feral pigeon

Who are birders and twitchers?

Birders and twitchers are names given to people who watch birds as a pastime. Birdwatching equipment includes a pair of binoculars and a notepad to sketch the birds that cannot be identified. There are hundreds of nature reserves around the world where people can go to watch birds.

Red-billed quelea

Red-headed quelea

Are some birds pests?

In central and southern Africa, the red-billed quelea occurs in massive flocks. A seedeater, it devastates precious crops. It is estimated that the world's 1.5 billion red-billed queleas need about 4,500 tonnes of food a day. Local people kill millions of the birds every year to keep the menace at bay. The red-billed quelea's close relative, the red-headed quelea, is not a pest. It has become rare and is now protected in many areas.

What is an ornithologist?

An ornithologist is a scientist who studies birds. Famous ornithologists include American John J. Audubon (1785–1851) and Englishman Peter Scott (1909–1989). Audubon was famous for travelling around the USA painting every species of bird. The National Audubon Society, which is dedicated to bird conservation in the USA, was named in his honour. Scott is remembered for his pioneering conservation work, and in particular for saving the ne-ne, a type of goose, from extinction.

What is falconry?

Falconry is a sport practised since ancient times using trained falcons to catch other birds and animals. The falcons are taken from their nests as chicks and trained by expert falconers.

Quick-fire Quiz

1. What is a twitcher?
a) A type of bird
b) A bird keeper
c) A birdwatcher

2. Who was Sir Peter Scott?
a) A falconer
b) An ornithologist
c) A twitcher

3. How many red-billed queleas are there in the world?
a) 15 million
b) 150 million
c) 1.5 billion

4. Which bird has a particular liking for the city?
a) Chicken
b) Quelea
c) Feral pigeon

Who keeps birds?

People in almost every country in the world keep birds as pets. The most popular are members of the parrot family, such as macaws (left), African greys and budgerigars, which are loved for their bright colours and ability to mimic human words. Songbirds are also popular. In places like Brazil and Spain, cities ring to the songs of caged birds. Sadly, trapping for the pet trade has led to the decline of many wild species.

How many chickens are there in the world?

Chickens are the most economically important bird worldwide, providing meat and eggs for millions of people. An estimate in 1999 concluded that there were over 13.2 billion chickens worldwide.

Threats to Birds

While birds overcome natural perils every day, they face greater threats from people. As our population expands, we take or destroy more and more of the world's natural habitats for our own use. Conservationists try to lessen the damage to our planet so that people, birds and other animals can live together.

What are the greatest dangers facing the world's birds?

Each type of bird, like any animal, needs a particular type of habitat in which to live. When people cut down forests for wood (right), flood unique valleys to create reservoirs or build roads across wild meadows, a piece of precious wildlife habitat and the animals that live within it are lost forever.

Is modern farming a problem?

Since the 1970s, farmers have developed ways to produce more crops and livestock. Unfortunately, some of the methods have drastically harmed wildlife, particularly birds. These measures include changes to when and how crops are sown, excessive use of pesticides and fertilisers, and the destruction of hedgerows. In Britain, populations of farmland birds have fallen by up to 90 per cent since 1975.

Do cats kill birds?

Although cats make good pets, they are highly efficient hunters and, in Britain for example, may kill as many as 70 million garden birds a year. Some owners put bells on their cat's collar, which ring as the cat moves and warn birds that they are in danger.

What effect do oil spills have on wildlife?

Every year, leaks from shipwrecked oil tankers or broken pipelines pollute large stretches of coastline, killing all the marine life in that area. Seabirds such as gulls, guillemots and puffins become coated in oil as they hunt for food. Despite clean-up operations, most of these birds die. The affected coasts and seas take years to recover.

How can people help birds?

Conservation organizations such as the Royal Society for the Protection of Birds (RSPB) have successfully saved several species of birds from extinction. After rescuing the osprey in Scotland, the RSPB is introducing this once common bird back to English lakes. The birds are provided with food and artificial nests to help them breed (right). Most countries have societies that try to protect birds, and almost all of these rely on donations from the public.

Which birds have disappeared forever?

Sadly, conservation programmes arrived too late to save some birds. Over 114 species of bird have become extinct since the 1600s, including the dodo, the passenger pigeon and the great auk. The great auk was a large flightless seabird. It was killed for food and also because people thought it was a witch! The last pair died in 1844. Today, about 970 species of birds are in danger.

Great auk

Who shoots migrating birds?

In the southern Mediterranean, particularly in Italy, Malta and Cyprus, people shoot or trap migrating birds for sport. The annual total of kills is thought to be about 900 million birds. This wasteful massacre includes swallows, skylarks and other birds killed for fun and not for food. In some areas, seagulls are machine gunned from boats. Hunters in Malta kill up to 100,000 birds of prey a year.

Quick-fire Quiz

1. What is the greatest threat to birds?
a) Hunting
b) Loss of habitat
c) Cats

2. When did the great auk die out?
a) 1984
b) 1944
c) 1844

3. Which birds are most affected by oil spills?
a) Seabirds
b) Garden birds
c) Migrating birds

4. How many species of birds are in danger?
a) About 114
b) About 550
c) About 970

Index

alarm calls 26
albatrosses 5, 24, 25, 34
anhinga 11

bathing 9
beaks and bills 10–11, 30
birds of paradise 28
birds of prey 12, 13, 14, 18, 19, 23
birdwatching 36
bluethroat 26
bowerbird 28
brains 5
breeding 26, 28, 29, 32–33
budgerigars 26, 37

camouflage 8, 25, 28
cassowaries 20
chickens 32, 33, 37
chicks 12, 24, 32, 33, 34–35
colonies 31
colours 8, 10, 14, 25, 28
condors 19
conservation 37, 39
crows 5, 9, 35
cuckoos 31, 34
curlews 10

dangers 38–39
dawn chorus 27
displays 28–9
dodo 21
ducks 12, 14, 18, 31
dunlin 22

eagles 10, 13, 17, 30, 32
eggs 32–33, 37
egrets 28
emu 20
extinct birds 4, 6–7, 21, 39

falcons 14, 18
falconry 37
feathers 6, 8–9, 11, 24, 28, 34
feet and talons 12–13
finches 5, 13, 16, 30, 32, 33
flamingo 8, 10
flightless birds 20–21
flocks 22, 36
flying 5, 18–19, 22, 34
food and feeding 10, 11, 16–17,
    20, 21, 25, 34, 35
frigate bird 18, 29

gannet 31
gizzards 16
geese 12, 18, 22, 37
grebes 29, 35
guillemots 25, 32, 38

habitats 24–25, 38
hearing 14, 15, 20
herons 17, 19
hoatzin 12
hummingbirds 4, 9, 19, 30

kakapo 21, 26
kingfisher 17

kiwi 20, 33
lily trotter 13

macaw 37
malleefowl 30, 32, 35
meadowlark 26
migration 22–23, 39
mimics 26, 27

nests and nesting 28, 30–31, 34
nightingale 27

oilbird 15
ornithologists 37
osprey 39
ostrich 4, 12, 13, 15, 20, 33
ovenbird 31
owls 14, 15, 25
oxpecker 16

parrots 21, 26, 34, 37
passerines 5
peafowl 8, 29
pelicans 11, 35
penguins 25, 35
people and birds 17, 20, 21,
    36–37, 38–39
pests 36
petrels 24, 25
pets 37
pigeons 9, 19, 23, 36
preening 10, 11
ptarmigan 25

puffin 24, 25, 38
queleas 36

rhea 20, 21
roadrunner 13
robins 5, 15

sandgrouse 24
seabirds 24, 25, 29, 31, 38, 39
seagulls 12, 24, 39
sight 14, 15
singing 26–27, 37
size 4
smell 20, 25
sparrows 36
speed 18, 20, 25
stonechat 26
survival 22, 24–25, 35
swallows 23, 31, 34, 39
swans 4, 9, 12, 20
swifts 19, 31

tailorbird 30
terns 23, 31
toucans 10

vultures 16, 19

warblers 5, 27, 34
wings 18, 19, 20
woodcock 8
woodpeckers 11
wrens 24, 27

Quick-fire Quiz ANSWERS

Page 5 World of Birds
1. c 2. a 3. c 4. a

Page 7 Early Birds
1. b 2. a 3. b,c 4. c

Page 9 Feathers
1. c 2. b 3. c 4. a

Page 11 Bills and Beaks
1. b 2. a 3. b,c 4. c

Page 13 Talons and Feet
1. b 2. a 3. c 4. a

Page 15 Sight and Sound
1. c 2. c 3. a 4. b

Page 17 Food and Feeding
1. a 2. c 3. b 4. c

Page 19 Flying
1. a 2. b 3. b 4. c

Page 21 Flightless Birds
1. b 2. b 3. a 4. c

Page 23 Migration
1. a 2. c 3. b 4. b

Page 25 Surviving Extremes
1. b 2. c 3. c 4. a

Page 27 Birdsong
1. b 2. c 3. c 4. a

Page 29 Displays
1. a 2. a 3. b 4. a

Page 31 Nests and Nesting
1. a 2. c 3. b 4. a

Page 33 Eggs
1. c 2. b 3. a 4. a

Page 35 Chicks and Young
1. a 2. c 3. b 4. b

Page 37 Birds and People
1. c 2. b 3. c 4. c

Page 39 Threats to Birds
1. b 2. c 3. a 4. c